THE JOURNEY OF THE MAYFLOWER

Andrea P. Smith

PowerKiDS
press
New York

Published in 2012 by The Rosen Publishing Group, Inc.
29 East 21st Street, New York, NY 10010

First Edition

Editor: Joanne Randolph
Book Design: Planman Technologies
Illustrations: Planman Technologies

Library of Congress Cataloging-in-Publication Data

Smith, Andrea P.
  The journey of the Mayflower / by Andrea P. Smith. — 1st ed.
      p. cm. — (Jr. graphic Colonial America)
  Includes index.
  ISBN 978-1-4488-5186-7 (library binding) — ISBN 978-1-4488-5210-9 (pbk.) —
ISBN 978-1-4488-5211-6 (6-pack)
  1. Mayflower (Ship)—Juvenile literature. 2. Pilgrims (New Plymouth Colony)—
Juvenile literature. 3. Massachusetts—History—New Plymouth, 1620–1691—
Juvenile literature. 4. Mayflower (Ship)—Comic books, strips, etc. 5. Pilgrims
(New Plymouth Colony)—Comic books, strips, etc. 6. Massachusetts—
History—New Plymouth, 1620–1691—Comic books, strips, etc. 7. Graphic
novels. I. Title.
  F68.S587 2012
  974.4'02—dc22
                                                              2011001705

Manufactured in the United States of America
CPSIA Compliance Information: Batch #PLS1102PK: For Further Information contact Rosen Publishing, New York,
New York at 1-800-237-9932

CONTENTS

MAIN CHARACTERS

William Bradford (1590–1657) Second governor of the Plymouth **Colony** and signer of the **Mayflower Compact**. He wrote a book about the **Pilgrims** called *Of Plymouth Plantation*.

William Brewster (1567–1644) One of the **founders** of the **Separatist** church. He signed the Mayflower Compact and became a church elder in Plymouth.

John Carver (1576–1621) First governor of the Plymouth Colony and signer of Mayflower Compact. He died during his first term, less than a year after he became governor.

Captain Christopher Jones (1570–1622) The captain of the *Mayflower*. He owned one-quarter of the ship.

Myles Standish (1584–1656) A soldier who met the Pilgrims in Holland. He helped the Pilgrims and guided them on **military** matters.

THE JOURNEY OF THE *MAYFLOWER*

IN ENGLAND IN 1607, EVERYONE HAD TO BELONG TO THE CHURCH OF ENGLAND. IT WAS THE LAW. A GROUP OF PEOPLE CALLED SEPARATISTS WANTED TO PRACTICE THEIR OWN RELIGION, THOUGH.

THEY BROKE THE LAW AND **WORSHIPPED** IN SECRET. THESE PEOPLE WOULD LATER BECOME KNOWN AS PILGRIMS.

4

5

THE TRIP TO THE NEW WORLD WAS HARD FOR THE PILGRIMS. THEY HAD TO STAY BETWEEN DECKS, OR BELOW THE MAIN DECK, FOR THE ENTIRE JOURNEY.

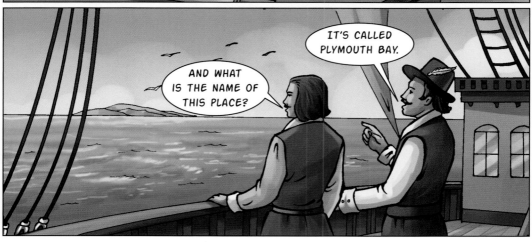

16

WE NEED A GOVERNMENT OR THIS COLONY WILL FAIL.

AYE.

THE PILGRIMS DRAFTED A **CONTRACT** LISTING ALL THE LAWS OF THEIR NEW COLONY. IT WAS CALLED THE MAYFLOWER COMPACT.

JUST SIGN HERE, MR. BRADFORD.

IT WILL BE MY PLEASURE.

18

21

TIMELINE

1534	King Henry VIII separates the Church of England from the Catholic Church.
1606	King James I allows the Virginia Company to build a settlement in North America.
1608	The Separatists escape to Holland.
Winter 1616	The Pilgrims talk about leaving Holland for the New World.
Summer 1617	Pilgrim leaders talk to the Virginia Company about moving to the New World and forming a colony.
Spring 1620	Pilgrim leaders make a deal with London investors so they can pay for their trip.
August 5, 1620	The *Mayflower* and the *Speedwell* begin their journey to the New World.
August 1620	The *Speedwell* leaks and has to be abandoned.
September 6, 1620	The *Mayflower* sets sail for the New World without the *Speedwell*.
November 9, 1620	The *Mayflower* reaches Cape Cod, Massachusetts.
November 22, 1620	Forty-one men sign the Mayflower Compact.
December 9, 1620	The Pilgrims find a suitable place to build their colony near Plymouth Bay.

GLOSSARY

abandon (uh-BAN-dun) To leave something or somewhere without planning to come back.

capsize (KAP-syz) To become overturned.

colony (KAH-luh-nee) A new place where people move that is still ruled by the leaders of the country from which they came.

contract (KAHN-trakt) An agreement between two or more people.

debt (DET) Something owed.

founders (FOWN-durz) The people who start something, such as a town or club.

investors (in-VES-turz) People who give money for something they hope will bring them more money later.

Mayflower Compact (MAY-flow-er KOM-pakt) An agreement that stated the way the Plymouth Colony would be governed.

military (MIH-luh-ter-ee) The part of the government, such as the army or navy, that keeps its citizens safe.

morale (muh-RAL) The feelings of a person or a group about the work they are doing.

New World (NOO WURLD) North America and South America.

Pilgrims (PIL-grumz) The people who sailed on the *Mayflower* in 1620 from England to America in search of freedom to practice their own beliefs.

Separatist (SEH-pruh-tist) A person in a religious group that separated from the Church of England.

survive (sur-VYV) To live through.

worshipped (WUR-shupd) Paid great honor and respect to something or someone.

INDEX

WEB SITES

Due to the changing nature of Internet links, PowerKids Press has developed an online list of Web sites related to the subject of this book. This site is updated regularly. Please use this link to access the list:

www.powerkidslinks.com/JGCO/mayflow